CELEBRATING THE FAMILY NAME OF RICHARDSON

Celebrating the Family Name of Richardson

Walter the Educator

Silent Richardson Books
a WhichHead Entertainment Imprint

Copyright © 2024 by Walter the Educator

All rights reserved. No part of this book may be reproduced in any manner whatsoever without written permission except in the case of brief quotations embodied in critical articles and reviews.

First Printing, 2024

Disclaimer

This book is a literary work; the story is not about specific persons, locations, situations, and/or circumstances unless mentioned in a historical context. Any resemblance to real persons, locations, situations, and/or circumstances is coincidental. This book is for entertainment and informational purposes only. The author and publisher offer this information without warranties expressed or implied. No matter the grounds, neither the author nor the publisher will be accountable for any losses, injuries, or other damages caused by the reader's use of this book. The use of this book acknowledges an understanding and acceptance of this disclaimer.

Celebrating the Family Name of Richardson is a memory book that belongs to the Celebrating Family Name Book Series by Walter the Educator. Collect them all and more books at WaltertheEducator.com

USE THE EXTRA SPACE TO DOCUMENT YOUR FAMILY MEMORIES THROUGHOUT THE YEARS

RICHARDSON

In fields where wildflowers bloom and sway,

Celebrating the Family Name of

Richardson

The name of Richardson lights the way.

A name of strength, of heart, of will,

A family bound by love and skill.

From humble roots to skies above,

The Richardson name is built on love.

With every step, they've carved their mark,

Through days of light and nights so dark.

Their story woven deep in time,

A melody, a constant rhyme.

From ancient lands to modern days,

The Richardson name forever stays.

They are the ones who dared to dream,

Who faced the winds, who crossed the stream.

With hands that worked, with minds that soared,

The Richardson name is ever adored.

Celebrating the Family Name of

Richardson

In fields of gold and cities wide,

They walk with honor, side by side.

Through every trial, they stand as one,

Their hearts alight, like rising sun.

For Richardson means more than name,

It's spirit, drive, and unbound flame.

It's courage found in every heart,

A family strong, in every part.

From builders, thinkers, makers, too,

They've shaped the world, both old and new.

With hands that crafted, minds that led,

The Richardson path, forever tread.

Their roots go deep in soil and stone,

A legacy that's brightly grown.

Through generations, they have passed,

Celebrating the Family Name of

Richardson

A name that's built to truly last.

From quiet towns to cities tall,

The Richardson name has seen it all.

Through times of change, through peace and war,

Their spirit holds, forever more.

With every dawn, they rise anew,

Their hearts ablaze, their dreams in view.

For Richardson is more than sound,

It's every value, tightly bound.

ABOUT THE CREATOR

Walter the Educator is one of the pseudonyms for Walter Anderson. Formally educated in Chemistry, Business, and Education, he is an educator, an author, a diverse entrepreneur, and he is the son of a disabled war veteran. "Walter the Educator" shares his time between educating and creating. He holds interests and owns several creative projects that entertain, enlighten, enhance, and educate, hoping to inspire and motivate you. Follow, find new works, and stay up to date with Walter the Educator™

at WaltertheEducator.com

www.ingramcontent.com/pod-product-compliance
Lightning Source LLC
LaVergne TN
LVHW012052070526
838201LV00082B/3921